Barn Owls

Silent but Majestic!

Dr. Richard A. NeSmith

Love of Nature Series

ISSUE 18

Applied **P**rinciples of **E**ducation & *Learning*

APE-Learning

© 2020 Richard A. NeSmith
Love of Nature Series

dr.nesmith@gmail.com

http://richardnesmith.obior.cc

All images in this book are copyrighted by their respective photographers.

Dr. Richard A. NeSmith

May 2025

ISBN: 9798553541439

FLESCH-KINCAID GRADE LEVEL: 7.3

Barn Owls
(Tyto *alba*)

Owls are from the Class **Aves**, of which two groups exist (*Tytonidae* and *Strigidae*). Barn owls are of the former. There are a number of anatomical differences in these, but one of the most significant is the skull (see below). The name ***owl***

has roots in early European languages and attempted to describe the sound the birds made. Owls are found on every continent except Antarctica. The actual number

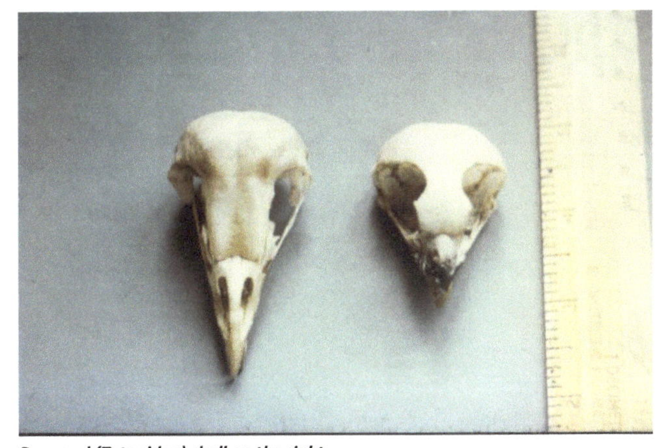

Barn owl (Tytonidae) skull on the right.

3

of species is unknown but reported to be from 130 to 200. Nineteen species of owls live in North America alone, of which 16 have been identified in southwestern British Columbia, Canada.

Some owls are limited to specific habitats, while others can quite adapt and survive in different environments. Each owl species seems to have its own uniqueness. The barn owl appears to be the best contender for the accolade, *silent but majestic*. They are seldom seen but magnificent to watch.

The barn owl is a species that has a total of thirty-something **subspecies** worldwide. Zoologists have not all agreed on precisely how to divide owls by species and sub-species.[1] So we will keep our focus more general and discuss these as a more unified group under the overarching umbrella of the genus-species **Tyto *alba***. Tyto in Greek means *owl,* and alba

---

[1] Debates are still ongoing about which barn owls constitute separate species and which are subspecies

means *white*. The barn owl is then, as named, the *white owl*, which nicely fits when one views this bird from the front.

Range

Barn owls are found in nearly every state in the US, including Hawaii, where it was introduced in 1958 to control rodents. Barn owls are the most widespread of all the North American owl species.[2] Also, these owls are prolific in the Americas and are thriving even in Central and South America.

Although young barn owls may scatter hundreds of miles from where they hatched, adult barn owls do not migrate seasonally.

Barn owl distribution in the US and parts of the Americas.

Characteristics

The barn owl is primarily white with yellow plumage and a yellowish-brown shade, with dark speckled freckles. The eyes and beak are entirely encircled by a *heart-shaped* facial **tuft** of white feathers rimmed with tan feathers. The tuft is feathers

---

[2] Barn owls were once considered the *most widely-distributed land bird in the world* being present on every continent except Antarctica.

around the neck raised in response to noise, essentially

enlarging the facial disc and improving hearing.

It is a magnificent bird and quite distinct from other types of owls. Owls are considered **raptors** or *birds of prey* because they use sharp **talons** (claws) and **curved bills** to hunt, kill, and eat other animals.

Their name originated from the rural and farmlands that once dotted our nation's landscape and how nearly every farm had a barn. And, yes, these owls favored those wooden barns and were regular residents. Unfortunately, most of those barns are now gone or replaced by fortressed metal barns.

Barn owls are medium-sized owls with long, sparsely feathered legs with grey toes. They are **solitary** or found in pairs. There is no specific name given to identify the male or female owl in English, though *hen* is sometimes used, as in hen-owl. This dilemma is probably because even experts find it almost impossible to determine the sex of a barn owl without veterinarian assistance. We know the

hen owl is slightly larger (weighing around 570 grams)[3] than the male (around 470 grams)[4] with darker legs. The female beak is buff-colored, whereas the males are more of an ivory color. Females weigh up to 1 lb. more than males, with a slightly wider wingspan (from 42.2-43.4 inches or 107-110 cm). These characteristics, however, are hard to notice upon

casual viewing.

The female barn owls plumage is also somewhat showier

---

[3] 20.2 ounces

[4] 16.6 ounces

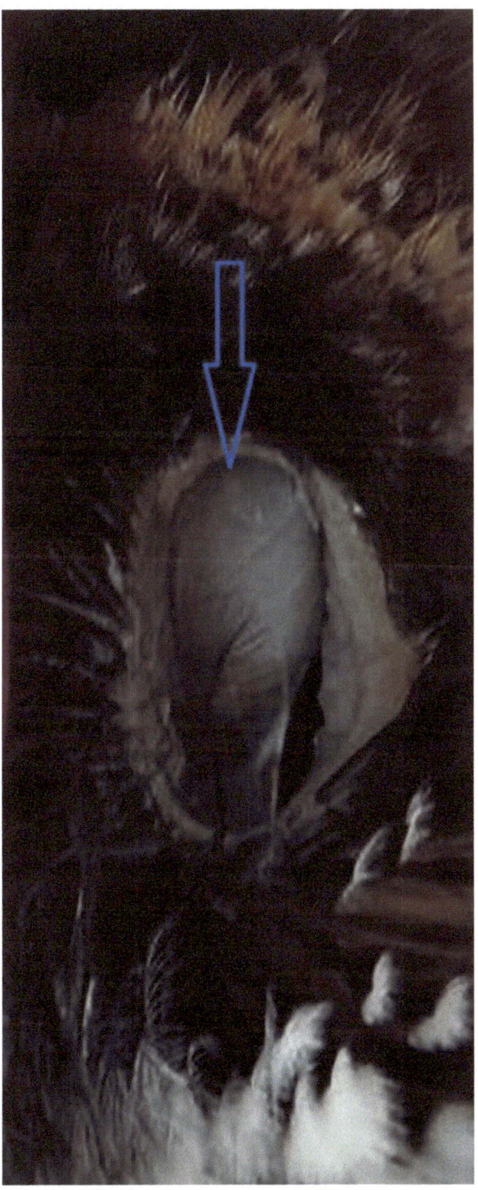

Moving the feathers to reveal the owl's ear opening.

than the males. Her feathers are more reddish and with a more heavily spotted chest. Some thought suggests the spottedness may indicate the quality and health of the bird. Heavily spotted females seem to be more resistant, in general, to parasites (such as flies, fleas, and mites) and diseases.[5] The spots may also be reproductive triggers that stimulate the male to help in nest-building.

The barn owl's most noticeable features are its ❶ heart-shaped looking face, ❷ large, rounded head, and ❸ enormous dark brown or black eyes. Then, of course, ❹ their ability for total soundless flight.

The head is large, round, and without tufts that look pointed on the horned

---

[5] Including some protozoan blood and intestinal parasites.

owl.[6] The wings also are rounded, and the tail is short and covered with white or light brown downy feathers. Though the bird's front is generally white, the head and dorsal (back) are light brown with black and white spots and scattered golden light brown. The underside of the wings is grayish-white.

The barn owl has two huge ear orbits (sockets) in the forehead of the skull. Both are covered with ear flaps (see arrow on the photograph). The holes (openings) are symmetrically placed and covered by tufts of feathers. However, the ear **flaps** that develop over them are not symmetrical. The owl's right ear flap opens slightly upward while its left ear opens slightly downward. This arrangement dramatically improves aim and calibration when setting one's sight during hunting. The left ear flap is more focused on the ground, whereas the right one is more attentive to what is just above the owl. As the hearing is so keen, an owl can locate its prey in the grass, swoop down, and grab it even in

---

[6] Tuft: A small collection of something, such as hairs. Some owls have these and they look pointed on the tips of the ears. Tufts on the end of the ears is characteristic of horned owls. The tufts on the barn owl are in the vicinity of the ear orbitals but not as noticeable as those of the horned owl.

the dark without any light.

Such keen hearing means the owl's ears are also extremely sensitive to sound and very loud noises. Not only would a loud noise scare them away, but it could damage their ears. An owl can close its feathered ear flaps under disturbingly noisy conditions if the sound intensity is too much.

Owls have a highly sensitive low-light vision. The owls' eyes are huge! An owl's eyes are enormous compared to their body and make up three percent of their body weight.[7] Their eyes are not *balls-in-sockets* like ours or most animals. Instead, they are *tube-shaped* eyes that are entirely immobile, encircled, and held rigidly in place by **bones** called ***sclerotic rings***.

A barn owl's vision is binocular (two eyes), providing excellent **depth perception** and relationships between objects. An owl's eye focuses entirely on its prey with a complete, accurate boost estimating distance. But, without the muscle to move their eyes to see, they must move their heads. This task is

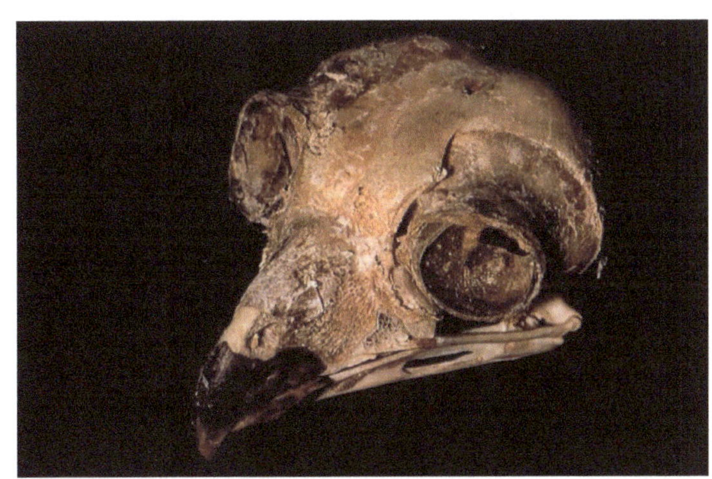

Bony sclerotic rings around the eyes holding them in place in an immobile manner. Courtesy of photographer, Connie Toops.

---

[7] In comparison, a human's eyes account for about .0003% of a human's body weight.

easily accomplished since owls can rotate their necks a maximum of 270 degrees without breaking blood vessels or tearing tendons. That's 75% of a circle.

Nictitating membrane clearly visible in both eyes in this owl.

In comparison, humans can only rotate the neck 80 to 90 degrees. This feat is accomplished by the owl possessing 14 **vertebrae** in its neck. That is twice as many as humans. Also, owls have only one *occipital articulation* with the cervical vertebrae (humans have two). This joint provides the ability to move the head separate from the body. Or, in other words, a joint that connects the head and the backbone. This single joint permits the owl to pivot on the vertebrae column, much like our body can pivot on one foot.

A barn owl's eyes and its ability to move its neck are essential characteristics for improving hunting skills. Owls have three eyelids. The upper eyelid closes downward when an owl blinks. The lower eyelid closes up as the owl sleeps. The third eyelid is called the **nictitating membrane**. It is especially useful in protecting the owl's eyes from injury while catching prey.

For owls, however, the ability to *locate prey by sound* is even keener. Astonishingly, their **acute sense of hearing** has

been tested. The results indicated that an owl can survive
and successfully hunt and capture prey by sound alone. One

might not see a mouse or vole in the dense vegetation, but owls don't need to. They can hear them at their exact location, whether they see them or not.

Some biologists have suggested that an owl can hear a beetle running through grass 100 feet away or a mouse squeaking at a distance of half a mile.[8] With the heart-shaped frame, the

face's design creates a *sound tunnel* and guides sound directly to the eardrums. Like a satellite dish collects and filters radio waves, the heart-shaped tunnel collects sound. Barn owls are the most accurate of all birds at locating prey by sound. With this *parabola-effect*, it allows the owl to detect the movement of its prey with complete accuracy.[9] With the tuft of hair, ear flaps, and ability to fine-tune turning the head, no wonder a

---

[8] Owl hearing is much more sensitive than that of other birds (it is more on the level of a cat's hearing), particularly at frequencies of 5 kHz and above. Barn Owls use sound frequencies above 8.5 kHz to direct and make an accurate strike at a prey item.

[9] A dish or cone is a parabola. The curved cone will collect the soundwaves facing its direction and focus them directly into the barn owl's ear.

barn owl can hear a mouse's heartbeat in a 30 square-foot room.

Diet

As we have discovered, owls are *nocturnal* (night-active) **carnivores**, focusing on hunting and eating meat. Though some owls have been observed to eat carrion, this has not been witnessed in barn owls. Barn owls capture and eat small animals such as insects, spiders, earthworms, snails, amphibians, reptiles, and crabs. Also, they *prefer* mice, voles, shrews, rats, muskrats, hares, and rabbits. They may occasionally prey on small birds. Their actual diet depends on the species of owl. Owls might consume several prey within a short period, then hunt again in 12 hours, but much more often if raising owlets.

The owl's digestive system is unique and will require further

attention to understand birds of prey better. The **pharynx** is the area between the mouth and the esophagus. The esophagus is a tube leading down from the pharynx and has circular and longitudinal muscles to permit swallowing. The owl does not have teeth, so they cannot chew their food. They do sometimes tear the prey into bits, but often they swallow it whole.

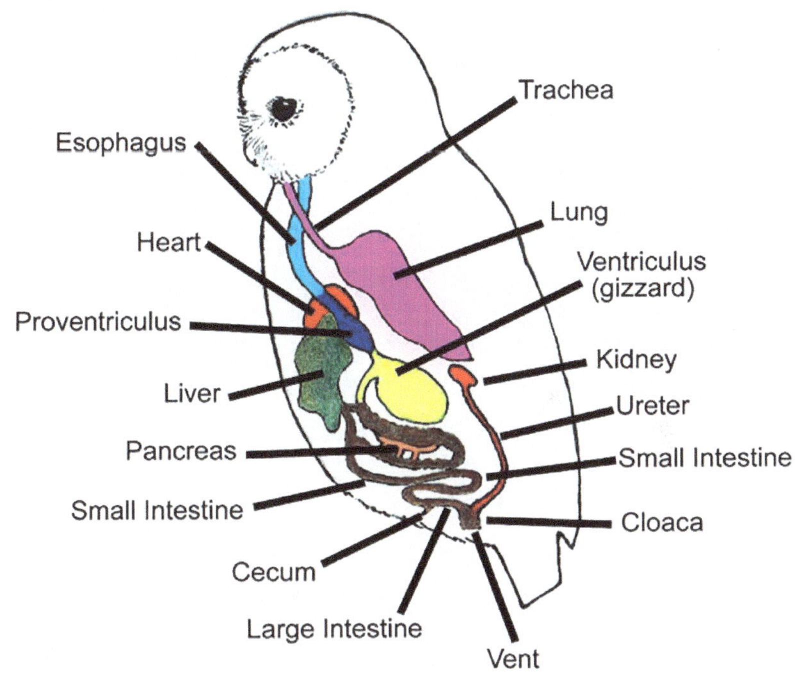

© Alan Sieradzki

The food would now travel to the crop in most birds, a loose sac in the throat that serves as storage for later consumption. But owls do not have a crop. So instead, the food travels down to the *two-chambered* **stomach**: the proventriculus and the gizzard.

Proventriculus (glandular stomach)

The proventriculus secretes an acid for breaking down food substances. This first-stage stomach is very well developed in birds, such as owls, that swallow entire fish and other small animals containing bones. A bird's stomach acid can have a pH of 2.2 to 2.5, similar to the

pH of lemon juice or vinegar. It's not a strong acid, so only soft tissue is digested (but no bones or fur). As a result, not all of the animal's swallowed are digested. But it is in the proventriculus that the acid is mixed with the food and digestive enzymes.

Gizzard

As food moves into the stomach, the liver and pancreas secrete digestive enzymes into the small intestine. Here, the food is absorbed into the body. The food moves from the acid/enzyme bath to the **gizzard**. The gizzard has no digestive glands. It has three main functions:

❶ As a filtration and absorption system where usable substances get moved into the bloodstream.

❷ It grinds up the meaty part of the meal as a very muscular organ, and finally, as a holding tank.

❸ Indigestible parts remain in the gizzard, mostly bones, teeth, fur, and scales (if fish have been eaten).

Nutrients leave the gizzard and are absorbed into the bloodstream, and then enter every cell of the body, where the mitochondria manufacture energy. Food bits remaining (bones, teeth, and fur) are compressed at the gizzard base, and after several hours, a pellet forms.[10] The pellet then moves back up into the owl's glandular stomach. It is the reverse muscle contractions (called **reverse peristalsis)** for swallowing. Spasms force the pellet up and into the esophagus for extraction. This process will last from a few seconds to several minutes.

Pellets may stay in the gizzard for a period of 10 to 12 hours. Pellets stored in the stomach partially block the owl's digestive system, and new prey cannot be swallowed until

---

[10] In falconry, the pellet is called a casting.

the pellet is ejected. Regurgitation often signifies that an owl is ready to eat again. An owl will cough up pellets twice a day rather than passing these through its digestive tract. Scientists use owl pellets to learn about owls, their diets, and their environment.

Should you already ask the question, the answer is "yes," owls have a large intestine, and they produce **excrement** (poop) and pellets. Though the food they eat does not pass entirely through their digestive tract, waste is still expelled.

Owl pellet contain bone, teeth, and animal skins, and scales if fish were consume. Courtesy of Alan Sieradzki, a senior researcher for Global Owl Project.

Habitat

Barn owls have a wide range of habitats, from rural to urban. Because of their diets, they are more often found at low elevations in open habitats. In America's early history, farmers built a door and box at the top of their barns just for owls. That custom has all but been

lost. They may live in very wooded forests, but often do their hunting in such places as grasslands, marshes, pastoral fields, farmlands, or even deserts. Adequate cavities for nesting seem to be determining factors, especially since the American landscape has changed, and most barns upgraded in less owl-friendly ways. Being **nocturnal**, owls roost during the day in barns, tree cavities, crevices in cliffs, riverbanks, nest boxes, church steeples, and other human-made structures.

Behavior

Barn owls are **solitary** or found in mating pairs. A group of owls is called a **parliament**. These owls begin hunting alone after sunset. As **predators**, barn owls are silent and hunt on floating wingbeats in open fields and meadows. An owl can approach its prey almost unnoticed (*stealth*). They hover like a fairy in the wind. Some have described them as hovering moths or hummingbirds. Only their wings need not have the motion or speed of the latter.

Compared to most birds, barn owls have a very *low wing loading* (large wings supporting a lightweight body). This ratio means they can fly very slowly without stalling and hover in only the slightest lift (rising air). As mentioned, stealth

capabilities arise from the softness and lack of oils on their feathers *and* the flight feathers' serrated (jagged) leading edges. (see photograph and pointer on page 23)[11] Their body

---

[11] As the jagged edges of the primary and secondary flight feathers reduced sound so much the aeroniautical industry/military has spent a great deal of time and money trying to determine how to apply this to sealth flight technology.

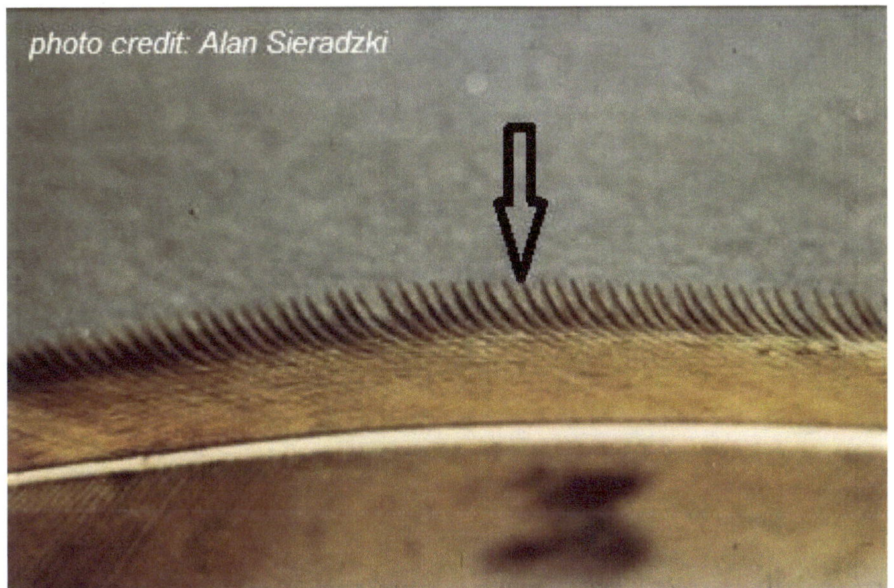

Serrated ends on the feathers improves aerodynamic performance and silent flight.

is light due to a lightweight skeletal system, which only takes 7-9% of their total body weight. Many of the larger bones are hollow, have bony internal braces, and are fused, giving them stronger support on the ground.

Barn owls do not ***hoot*** like other owls. You can find them by listening for their eerie, raspy calls, quite unlike other owls' hoots. Instead, they **screech**. It can sometimes sound like an angry, screaming toddler. Other sounds include hissing. Males might hiss to invite a female to inspect a nest site. Females might hiss to beg for food from the male. Barn owls also make a loud, 3-4 second hiss at intruders or predators that come too close or disturb their nest.

Additional sounds can be heard as barn owls communicate vocally. These include different utterances best described as twittering[12] to express discomfort, attention-seeking, or quarreling with nestmates. Young owlets also give off raspy/snoring calls when hungry. Probably the best-known sound is the one adults give off, sounding like a drawn-out garbling scream. These indicate distress if drawn-out. Giving an explosive yell directed at mammalian predators will usually be enough warning. Some sounds are greeting-specific for mates and courtship. However, barn owls are very quiet and elusive when not breeding.

In flight, they are light, aerodynamic, and seldom affected by the wind. The weather, however, does have its

restrictions. Their downy feathers help to muffle the sound of their movement. But the silence of the owl's flight is due to the very soft feathers and the lack of oils in them. This

---

[12] *Twittering*, in nature, is repeated light shaking or quivering sounds.

benefit, however, causes issues when it rains. It is rare to see an owl hunting in the rain. Other birds have feathers protected by the oils, but fail to provide them with a soundless flight. The fluffy feathers of an owl will soak up water like a sponge. A soaked owl is an unhappy owl, and wet owls can't fly in the rain very long. If they get wet, they generally will have to wait until they are dry enough to fly again.

While hunting, barn owls may hover or simply swoop down on their prey, attacking in low flight from 4.11-15 feet (1.5 m-4.5 m) above the ground. They then capture the prey with their powerful legs and **talons**, usually crushing the prey quickly (see photograph below). However, with larger animals, owls remove any danger by snipping through the back of the skull with the bill. Then they swallow the prey whole. Barn owls do cache extra food, especially during the

breeding season.

Barn owls are very efficient hunters. With advanced **senses** of *sight* and *hearing*, barn owls easily boast a kill rate of over 85%. That is far better than that of hawks and other raptors. Some people have mistakenly assumed barn owls are loafers, spending most of their time being sedentary and just sitting around looking. But being so effective and efficient enough at hunting has provided the barn owl a very different lifestyle than most wildlife.

Reproduction

Barn owls are commonly **monogamous**, meaning they will choose a mate for life. However, there are some reports that **polygamy** exists. Mating pairs typically remain together as long as both individuals live. Courtship initiates with

displayed flights by males. Such exhibitions are accompanied by calls advertising and chasing the female, with a great deal of screeching taking place by both. The demonstrations include the male hovering with his feet dangling in front of a

perched female for several seconds. These courting dances or flights are known as **moth flights.**

Barn owls typically breed only once per year but can breed almost any time of the year (depending upon food supply). Nest-building can be stimulated if rodent populations are on the rise. So, breeding is closely linked to food availability.

Breeding and copulation frequently occur during the searching period for an adequate nest. Both can solicit the breeding, as is indicated by crouching down or the spreading of the wings. Young owls begin breeding at one year of age. On average, barn owls usually raise one **brood** per year; however, some have raised up to three families in one year. As the lifespan of most individuals barn owls is only *two years*, they typically only breed once or twice. The oldest living barn owl in captivity is Barnaby, the barn owl. At 26, this resident of the Ohio Wildlife Center might be the oldest living barn owl ever.

Barn owls have specific requirements for an acceptable nest. However, it is not uncommon for them to choose an old nest that has been used for decades rather than to build a new one. The female usually lines the nest with shredded pellets. Two to 18 eggs can be laid, though usually, four to seven is average. Eggs are laid two to three days apart, explaining the need for frequent mating. The female incubates the eggs for 29 to 34 days. The chicks, hatching on different days, are born helpless and naked.

 The female eats the chicks' feces for the first few weeks after hatching in order to keep the nest sanitized.[13] The timing and straddling of the chicks' ages is by design. This timing appears to ensure their survival chances as they are fed in their hatching-seniority order. This spacing ensures success for all, that is, except for the last born, who quite possibly will die and its carcass consumed by its siblings. Since the female does all the brooding, she only leaves the nest during incubation for very short periods. The male provides food for all while the females do the feeding, initially tearing the food into small pieces.

---

[13] Nest maintenance is importants as nestlings are commonly infested with the dipteran Carnus *hemapterus*, blood-sucking ectoparasites of nestling birds.

This parental feeding period can last for 25 days following hatching. The first nest *flight* occurs between 50 and 70 days after hatching, and they will continue to return to the nest to roost for another seven to eight weeks. Within the first three to five weeks, young owlets become independent and feed themselves.

Miscellaneous

We know that owls sleep during daylight hours. We also know that adult owls sleep upright. However, the head of a young owlet is too heavy to sleep upright. So they can sleep lying down on their stomachs with their head turned to the side. Once the owlet's neck muscles are more fully developed, they begin to sleep like adults.

Nocturnal animals have

eyes that are rich in **rods**, which explains their keen night vision. Owl's eyes are dominated by densely packed retinal rods. All animal eyes have photo-receptors called **cones** and rods. Retinal cones function best in bright light and provide color vision. Rods are much more sensitive and perform best in dim lights. Rods outnumber cones 30 to 1 in owl species, including the great horned owl and barn owl, enabling them to see better than humans in nighttime darkness.

Also, many animals have a layer of tissue behind the retina that reflects visible light. This coating is called the **tapetum lucidum** and reflects light entering the eye. It dramatically increases the light available to the photoreceptors, improving night vision. At night, this reflection can be seen by shining a flashlight into an animal's eyes. It is referred to as *eyeshine*, and for an owl, the color reflected is red.

Barn owls seem to have a relatively simple and short life despite the highly adaptive traits that make them such a successful predator. Barn owls themselves have very few predators. Occasionally, weasels and snakes take nestlings, and there is evidence that horned owls prey upon adult barn owls. However, owls have a resilient **defense mechanism**. Upon recognizing a threat, barn owls spread their wings tilted down towards the intruder. This increases the

appearance of their size. They then sway their heads back and forth, hissing, squinting, and snapping their bills. If this doesn't scare off the invader, the owl will fall back and strike with its feet.

Having learned that barn owls are

far more effective hunters than most animals, it seems ironic that the barn owls' lifespan is rather short. But, their brooding once or twice ensures the species' continuance. Most barn owls die young. Of those that fledge,[14] nearly

---

[14] *Fledgling* is a word used to describe the period of time it takes to develop wing feathers that are large enough for flight. One who reaches this stage is then referred to as a *fledgling*.

70% die in their first year.

In one study of over 8,000 barn owls that carried identi-fication bands (rings), it was found that the average lifespan of those above five weeks old is just less than 18 months. The **mortality rate** of nestlings is not even considered. Getting from the nest to the first self-feeding seems to be a milestone, followed only by the high death rate for those having left to establish their own territory in that first year (called **juvenile dispersal**). Inexperience is costly for the new young owls when trying to venture on their own.

A barn owl's range is very dynamic due to the juvenile's strong dispersal instinct, which scatters them up to hundreds of miles in all directions. This distribution practice means

that those areas available receive young barn owls regularly. If proper habitat and nesting sites are accessible, then there is a good chance those barn owls will try to populate those areas.

The leading cause of death in barn owls is **starvation**, typically of inexperienced young birds during juvenile dispersal or severe winter weather periods. Other reasons involve the poisoning/pesticides of rodents consumed by barn owls by farmers, landowners, and even local businesses.[15] These chemicals are anticoagulants and cause internal bleeding. Other agricultural techniques used to exterminate vermin reduce that which owls would typically

---

[15] For reasons still unknown, barn owls suffer more severe effects from consuming pesticides than other species of owls (especially rat posion). It has been noted that DDT and other pesticides are often responsible for the thinning of eggshell in females. Currently, DDT is not permitted to be used in the USA unless for public health emergencies, such as controlling a vector disease.

consume.

Also, owls are susceptible to disease and parasites and organisms that are possibly infectious to humans. Barn owls are furthermore vulnerable to protozoan blood and intestinal parasites and two species of lice. However, the likelihood of a person contracting a disease from an owl is rare.

Other factors that threaten barn owls include injury or death by flying into power lines (electrocution), climate changes, and potential habitat loss, including fewer nesting options. Barn owls are declining in some parts of their range despite a worldwide distribution due to habitat loss. Climate changes in northern regions also cause snow to accumulate and last longer, making winter survival long and more difficult for the species. Unlike most other birds, barn owls do not store up extra fat in their bodies as a winter reserve. This lack of insulating fat causes many owls to die during freezing periods. Or, they are simply too weak to breed during the coming spring.

Also, there are inadequate amounts of structures for nesting in modern farms. As a result, some farmland can no longer support a sufficient rodents population to feed a barn owl pair. The barn owl population, however, is declining only in some communities, not throughout the range.

Sighting barn owls is a unique and exciting opportunity. They are usually quiet and silent and generally stay hidden by shadows from their camouflage-speckled backs. However, there are encounters in which the two can be very vocal to one another, much as in a contentious conversation. As such, throughout history, they have been connected to folklore and superstition. Some see them as a bad **omen**. In most Native American tribes, owls are a symbol of *death*. Others see them as a sign of *wisdom*.

There are no adverse effects of barn owls on humans; however, owls of all kinds have been known to attack people when defending their young, mates, or territories. Frequent targets include unwary joggers and hikers. However, often victims escape *without* injury, and deaths from owl attacks are extremely rare. In addition, barn owls seem to pose no threat to most dogs or cats.[16]

Barn owls serve a purpose in their ecosystems. First, they limit populations of the mammal and bird species upon which they prey. Second, they serve as food for those other **predator** species.

In summary, barn owls are some of the most unique birds of prey on the planet. They do provide a service in that they limit rodent pest populations, benefiting farmers and others. Barn owls are protected under the U.S. Migratory Bird Treaty Act[17] and other federal and local statutes. Though thriving in some ecosystems, populations are generally small. In some states, they are considered endangered, such as in Michigan. It appears that the Great

---

[16] Of course, all small pets should be properly attended and watched if outside or in the forest.

[17] See: https://www.fws.gov/birds/policies-and-regulations/laws-legislations/migratory-bird-treaty-act.php

Lake states (plus Iowa and Missouri) are suffering the most barn owl population losses at this time. Overall, they are not federally **threatened** or **endangered** in the United States, but they are protected in many states.

Since a lack of nesting opportunities seems to be such a fundamental cause of barn owl demise, building an **owl box** or home has become a popular way to help barn owls continue. It is also a means of drawing barn owls into one's neighborhood, putting them in charge of pest control.

These are very quiet, very private birds of prey. They are seldom seen by humans and yet provide a great service in keeping rodent populations in check. Moreover, their manner of silent hunting is nothing short of awe-inspiring to watch. They are, indeed, *silent but majestic*.

REVIEW

1. Tyto *alba* is the genus species for the barn owl. What do these two Greek stems mean?

2. Explain what is meant by a bird *fledgling*?

3. What percentage of barn owls die once they fledge?

4. What is the proventriculus, and what purpose does it serve?

5. What does the word *brood* mean, and how many broods does a barn owl average?

6. What enables the barn owl to be able to fly in complete silence*?*

7. Many cultures have folklore surrounding the barn owl. What two different ways are these birds viewed?

8. Explain what *eyeshine* is and why it occurs?

9. Someone tells you they are afraid of barn owls attacking their poodle. What do you tell them?

10. What is one way to attract barn owls to your community?

BARN OWL

COLORING PAGE

http://www.supercoloring.com/coloring-pages/barn-owl

Name:________________________

Barn Owls: Silent but Majestic

Carefully read each question or clue. Record the answer in the appropriate boxes. Use the word bank if necessary.

solitary   parabola   rain   parliament   talons   gizzard   camouflage   nictitating   habitat

rods   owlets   pellets   Antarctica   Hawaii   screech   flaps

Across

3. Barn owls cannot digests an entire animal, so ______ form and are regurgitated.
5. Cells that help animals see better in the dark?
8. Digestive organ that attempts to grind up food parts.
9. Word describing baby owls?
11. Like most wildlife, ________ loss seems to threatens a species survival.
13. Barn owls are found on every continent except _________.
15. This can stop a barn owl from hunting?
16. Barn owls hunt ______________.

Down

1. Protests a barn owl's ears.
2. Where barn owls was introduced in 1958 to control rodents?
4. Barn owls don't 'hoot,' they _______.
6. heart-shaped looking face creates a _____________ effect.
7. __________________ membrane is another word for eyelids.
10. Name used to describe a group of owls.
12. Barn owl's plumage provides _______________.
14. Another word for 'claws.'

INTERESTING SOURCES TO CONSIDER

All About Birds: Barn Owls. Available at:
https://www.allaboutbirds.org/guide/Barn_Owl/overview

An Introduction to the Barn Owl. Available at:
https://youtu.be/ohqEquNnzfU

Barn Owl Chick Hatches: Super Powered Owls. BBC. Available at: https://youtu.be/weOKOzVi2jE

Barn Owl Facts. Available at:
https://www.barnowltrust.org.uk/barn-owl-facts/

Cute Barn Owl Learns How To Fly: Super Powered Owls. BBC. Available at: https://youtu.be/3C7do93-GB8

Digestion in Owls. Available at:
https://www.owlpages.com/owls/articles.php?a=4

Experiment! How Does An Owl Fly So Silently? Super Powered Owls: BBC. Available at: https://youtu.be/d_FEaFgJyfA

Graceful Barn Owl Hunting in the Daytime. BBC Earth. Available at: https://youtu.be/M-a6QjHrI_c

Guide to North American Birds: Barn Owls. Audubon. Available at: https://www.audubon.org/field-guide/bird/barn-owl

How Does An Owl's Hearing Work? Super Powered Owls. BBC. Available at: https://youtu.be/8SI73-Ka51E

Owl Ears. Available at:
https://www.internationalowlcenter.org/blog/owl-ears

Owls. Available at: https://bit.ly/2FRrZAS

Slow-Mo Barn Owl in Flight. Unexpected Wilderness: BBC Earth. Available at: https://youtu.be/hlKo42iPslg

The Private Life of the Barn Owl (David Attenborough). Available at: https://youtu.be/5NLFLO8LN78

ABOUT THE AUTHOR

Richard NeSmith is a native of Florida, USA. He grew up wading through the swamps of central Florida with his two younger brothers during the pre-Disney era, and unknowingly, falling in love with biology, wildlife, and nature. He has lived in seven American states, twice in Australia, and once in Mexico City. He holds eight university degrees and has taught for 14 years in secondary schools, here and abroad, and another 13 years as a professor in several American universities. His service includes professor of science education, Dean of Education, Campus Dean, and an online instructor. His passion for learning (and *how we learn*) did not develop until *after* graduating from high school. His only explanation for this is that *having a goal made all the difference in the world*. He enjoys reading, hiking, nature photography, golf, tennis, and RV camping.

http://richardnesmith.obior.cc

Applied Principles of Education & Learning *presents*

***APE*-Learning**

AMAZON AUTHOR's PAGE:

https://www.amazon.com/author/richardnesmith

Educational, wildlife, and naturalist books
Dr. Richard NeSmith.

Issue 1
Raccoons:
Friendly Bandits
Dr. Richard NeSmith

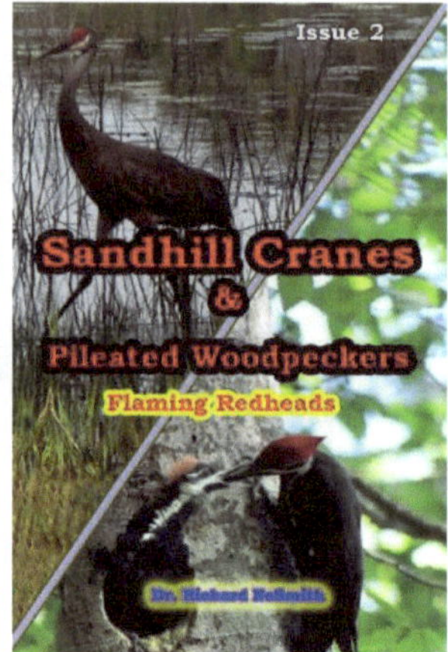
Issue 2
Sandhill Cranes
&
Pileated Woodpeckers
Flaming Redheads
Dr. Richard NeSmith

Issue 3
American
Alligators
&
Crocodiles
Dr. Richard NeSmith

Issue 4
Bobcats:
Ghostly Elusive
Dr. Richard NeSmith

Issue 5
Foxes:
Sneaky Rascals
Dr. Richard NeSmith

Issue 6
Armadillo:
Little Armored One
Dr. Richard NeSmith

Issue 7
Squirrels:
Bushy-Tail Scampers
Dr. Richard NeSmith

Issue 8
River Otters:
Aquatic Clowns!
Dr. Richard NeSmith

Issue 9
Beavers:
Nature's Engineers!
Dr. Richard NeSmith

Issue 10
Black Bears
Titans of the Forest
Dr. Richard NeSmith

Issue 11
Freshwater
Turtles
Dr. Richard NeSmith

Issue 12
FUNGI, LICHENS
& MUSHROOMS
Dr. Richard NeSmith

Paperbacks: http://amazon.com/author/richardnesmith

e-books: https://bit.ly/3iuCgB3

Special thanks to the following who kindly provided permission to use their photographs.

From Unsplash: Dave Lowe   **Flickr:** Lynn Griffiths

From FreeImages: Bruce Brouwer, bugdog, and Pamela Benn.

From Pixabay: Andreas Metallerreni, Pexels, makeitsomarketing, Herbert Aust, Mochamad Arief, David Borrill, usanne Jutzeler, LynnB, Danny Moore, Kevinsphotos, Peter Hoare, bugdog, John MacKinnon, Susanne Jutzeler, Petr Elvis, Rick Veldman, Lubos Houska, Janine Wilkins, Simone Dutt, Frank Gayde, Manfred Richter, Friedhelm Brandenburg, Steve Bidmead, Vicki Roberts, *and the prolific* skeeze.

Also, special thanks to **Alan Sieradzki**, a senior researcher for *Global Owl* Project for graciously providing several useful and insightful illustrations and the photographs for this project; **Mack Hitch** for the eyelid photo, to International Owl Center for the owl ear flap photo, (https://www.internationalowlcenter.org/blog/owl-ears) and **Connie Toops** for the barn owl skull. Thanks to International Owl Center for the owl ear flaps.

Thank you, everyone.

Love Learning – Love Nature – Love Life